Eng Grammar

AGE 9-11

Boswell Taylor

As a parent, you can play a major role in your child's education by your interest and encouragement. This book is designed to give your child an understanding of the rules of English grammar. Confidence in the basic principles of English will help improve your child's work in other school subjects.

The book introduces each part of speech in turn, with exercises to practise each point. There is a test to check your child's understanding before moving on to the next part of speech. Answers for all the exercises and tests can be found at the back of the book. Over the page you will find advice on how to help your child get the most out of this book.

Hodder Children's Books

NCPTA

The only home learning programme supported by the NCPTA

How to help your child

- Make sure your child completes all the exercises for each grammar point. The rules themselves are quite abstract, and the best way to learn them is through plenty of practice.

- If you find your child is getting answers wrong, don't make a big issue out of it. Simply talk through the relevant grammar point to make sure it has been fully understood, then suggest your child has another go at the exercises.

- Always take a positive approach, and concentrate on your child's successes by giving praise and encouragement.

- A good dictionary is an excellent investment which will help your child to make the best use of this book. Your child's teacher or a local bookseller or librarian may be able to recommend one.

Published by Hodder Children's Books 1995

10 9 8 7 6 5 4 3 2 1

ISBN 0 340 65109 1

Printed and bound in Great Britain

Hodder Children's Books
A division of Hodder Headline plc
338 Euston Road
London NW1 3BH

Previously published as Test Your Child's English Grammar

Facts about the parts of speech

We speak and write the English language. The structure that provides the word patterns is known as grammar. When we study grammar, we study how words are put together to form sentences. We rarely think about sentences or grammar when we speak and write. The words fall naturally into some sort of pattern. Sometimes the pattern is correct, and sometimes it is not. The use of correct grammar means that the correct meaning is conveyed. Incorrect grammar introduces confusion to the word patterns.

Word patterns are composed of parts of speech. Each part of speech has its own special function. There are eight (some say nine)* separate functions or jobs; there are eight parts of speech. Here they are:

Part of speech	Function	Examples
Noun	naming word	sausage, Jack
Pronoun	substitute for noun	she, he, it, they
Verb	doing word	walk, think
Adjective	describing word	proud, beautiful
Adverb	word modifying action	run *quickly*, work *late*
Preposition	relates one thing to another	ship *on* the sea, jump *over* the wall
Conjunction	joining word	the driver *and* the passenger
Interjection	expresses emotion	Oh! Ouch!

* Sometimes the three 'articles' *a, an* (indefinite) and *the* (definite) are called a part of speech.

Every word in this book and in every book belongs to one of the parts of speech.

Nouns

A noun is the name of a person, animal, place or thing. Everything has a name, such as **chair**, **ship**, **football**. Everybody has a name. There is the common name, such as **person**. **Boy** and **girl** are nouns to tell us the kind of **person**. Then every boy and every girl has a proper name, such as **William** or **Emma**. All the words printed here in bold type are nouns.

Underline each noun in the following sentences:

A 1 I patted a <u>dog</u>, stroked a <u>cat</u>, rode on an <u>elephant</u> and fed a <u>seal</u>.
  2 I sat on a chair, drank from a cup, ate off a plate and used a spoon.
  3 I played in the park, sailed a ship, built a sand-castle and flew a kite.
  4 I played football with William, John, Fred and Craig.

Write the most suitable noun from the list in each empty space:

snake, horse, lion, mouse, sparrow, frog

B 1 The ......*mouse*........ squeaked.   2 The ....neighed.
  3 The .... hissed.   4 The .... croaked.
  5 The .... chirped.   6 The .... roared.

Singular and Plural (Number)

Nouns can have either singular ('one') or plural ('more than one') number. Generally the plural is formed by adding **-s** or **-es** to the singular, but there are exceptions. In the exercise below, all the words are exceptions to the rule. Some words, like sheep, are both singular and plural.

Fill the gaps to complete the chart.

	Singular	Plural		Singular	Plural
C 1	knife	*knives*	2	....	thieves
3	child	....	4	....	geese
5	tooth	....	6	....	sheep

Nouns – Gender

Gender concerns the two sexes, male and female.
Masculine gender denotes the male sex, such as **man**, **father**, **boy**.
Feminine gender denotes the female sex, such as **woman**, **mother**, **girl**.
We also have Neuter gender and Common gender.
Neuter gender denotes things without sex, such as **ball**, **church**.
Common gender denotes either sex, such as **child**, **person**, **teacher**.

Fill the gaps to complete the chart:

	Masculine	Feminine		Masculine	Feminine
A	1 _abbot_	abbess	2	god	....
	3 grandfather	....	4	....	nun
	5	cow	6	gander	....
	7 emperor	....	8	....	lady
	9	princess	10	husband	....
	11 nephew	....	12	....	daughter
	13	ewe	14	stallion	....
	15 bridegroom	....	16	....	duchess
	17	landlady	18	uncle	....
	19 son-in-law	....	20	....	heiress

Change all masculines to corresponding feminines in the following:

B 1 The wizard changed the prince to a frog.

   The witch changed the princess to a frog. ....

2 The king awarded a medal to the hero.

   ....

3 The page followed the bridegroom into the church.

   ....

4 The policeman arrested the murderer.

   ....

5 The heir to the whole estate was a penniless actor.

   ....

Gender

Common gender words are unisex words. The same word is both male and female.
Neuter gender denotes non-living things that are neither male nor female.
Here are 49 nouns.   *Underline* the 24 words with Common gender.
                      Cross out the 25 words with Neuter gender.

A <u>child</u>   ~~chair~~   <u>friend</u>   <u>parent</u>   ~~school~~   <u>scholar</u>   <u>pig</u>
   house   mountain deer   volcano   singer   owner   window
   passenger pop-song explorer swimmer   ladder   radio   sheep
   fowl   boots   librarian desk   book   bird   ice-cream
   people   road   animal   sausage   onlookers balloon   choir
   rain   dagger   journalist mob   thunder   reader   coal
   car   canal   monarch   canoe   fish   door   lemonade

Families

A sheep can be a ewe (female), a ram (male) or a lamb (young animal).
These are the names (nouns) of the members of nine families all jumbled up:
**lion, bitch, foal, bull, mare, piglet, sow, stallion, duckling, drake, cock,
goose, cub, cow, buck, lioness, gosling, puppy, dog, gander, boar, calf,
duck, chick, fawn, hen, doe**

Use names from the list above to complete the chart to make happy families.

	Male	Female	Young animal
B 1	lion	lioness	cub
2	gander		
3			piglet
4		bitch	
5	drake		
6		mare	
7			fawn
8	bull		
9		hen	

Group Terms or Collective Nouns

A collective noun names a group of individuals as if they were one individual:

committee (of people)   **herd** (of cattle)   **pack** (of cards)

They may be singular or plural:

**one team of players   two teams of players
The committee is made up of boys and girls.
The committee are quarrelling among themselves again.**

Special group terms are used with both animate (living) and inanimate (non-living) things.
These are collective nouns:

crew, choir, flock, gang, company, swarm, litter, stud, shoal, school

Fill the gaps with the correct collective noun.

Animate (living things)

A 1 ...*litter*... of puppies   2 .... of sailors

3 .... of birds   4 .... of actors

5 .... of thieves   6 .... of whales

7 .... of herring   8 .... of singers

9 .... of horses   10 .... of bees

These are collective nouns:

library, suit, crate, fleet, bunch, bouquet, string, chest, bundle, set

Fill the gaps with the correct collective noun.

Inanimate (non-living things)

B 1 ...*bouquet*... of flowers   2 .... of books

3 .... of beads   4 .... of clothes

5 .... of grapes   6 .... of drawers

7 .... of tools   8 .... of ships

9 .... of rags   10 .... of fruit

★ Now test yourself in the use of nouns

Write the singular of the following:

A 1 children .... 2 geese .... 3 boxes ....

4 men .... 5 passers-by .... 6 teeth ....

Write the plural of the following:

B 1 woman .... 2 sheep .... 3 loaf ....

4 echo .... 5 mouse-trap .... 6 foot ....

Write the masculine equivalent of the following:

C 1 goddess .... 2 wife .... 3 bride ....

4 empress................ 5 niece .... 6 female ....

Write the feminine equivalent of the following:

D 1 lion .... 2 uncle .... 3 wizard ....

4 traitor .... 5 monk .... 6 headmaster ....

Complete the chart to make happy families:

Male	Female	Young	Male	Female	Young
E 1 leopard	....	2	sow		....
3 ram	....	4	....	calf	

Fill the gaps with the correct collective nouns.

F 1 .... of soldiers   2 ....of cattle

3 .... of sheep   4 .... of wolves

5 .... of lions   6 .... of geese

7 .... of mackerel   8 .... of furniture

Write the most appropriate word for a number of people:

G 1 at a music concert .... 2 in church ....

3 in a bus .... 4 in a supermarket ....

Write one word for a number of things:

H 1 .... of bananas   2 .... of bells

3 .... of strawberries 4 .... of islands

8

Pronouns

Pronouns are used in place of nouns. Look at these sentences:

Peter caught **the ball. Peter** bounced **the ball. Peter** kicked **the ball** upfield.

There is too much repetition. We can use 'he' instead of 'Peter' and 'it' instead of 'ball', like this:

Peter caught **the ball. He** bounced **it. He** kicked **it** upfield.

We cannot change the name 'Peter' to 'he' in the first sentence, or 'ball' to 'it' or we would not know to whom 'he' referred and to what 'it' referred. A pronoun must always have a noun nearby to which it refers.

There are seven personal pronouns. They are the 'doers':

I   you   he   she   it   we   they

Each one makes sense if it is used to complete this sentence: ....saw Louise.

I saw Louise.   **You** saw Louise.   **He** saw Louise.   **She** saw Louise.
It saw Louise.   **We** saw Louise.   **They** saw Louise.

Each of these 'doers' has a 'receiver'. Something happens to it.

me   you   him   her   it   us   them

Each one makes sense if it is used to complete this sentence:
Louise saw ....

In each of the following you are given the 'doer' (the subjective). Put the correct 'receiver' (the objective) in the gap.

A 1 I saw Louise. Louise saw ...*me*....   2 You saw Louise. Louise saw ....

   3 He saw Louise. Louise saw ....   4 She saw Louise. Louise saw ....

   5 It saw Louise. Louise saw ....   6 We saw Louise. Louise saw ....

   7 They saw Louise. Louise saw ....

Write these sentences. Use pronouns instead of the nouns shown in *italics*.

B 1 Duncan went to the circus. *Duncan* went with his friends.
       Duncan went to the circus. He went with his friends.

   2 Yasmin plays tennis. *Yasmin* is good at the game.

       ....

   3 The snake saw the bird. *The snake* glided away.

9

Each of the personal pronouns has a possessive pronoun. These are the 'owners':

Nominative ('doers'):	I	you	he	she	it	we	you	they
Objective ('receivers'):	me	you	him	her	it	us	you	them
Possessive ('owners'):	mine	yours	his	hers	its	ours	yours	theirs

Complete the following, adding the correct possessive pronouns:

A 1 I bought the bike. It is my bike. The bike is ....

   2 You bought the bike. It is your bike. The bike is ....

   3 He bought the bike. It is his bike. The bike is ....

   4 She bought the bike. It is her bike. The bike is ....

   5 The dog caught the ball. It is his ball. The ball is ....

   6 We bought the books. They are our books. The books are ....

   7 They bought the books. They are their books. The books are ....

We can add '**self**' or '**selves**' to a personal pronoun to make a compound pronoun. Such compound pronouns are called reflexive pronouns because they look back on themselves.

  myself yourself himself herself itself ourselves themselves

Complete the following, adding the correct reflexive pronoun:

B 1 I feed ...*myself*... 2 You feed .... 3 He feeds ....

   4 She feeds .... 5 It feeds .... 6 We feed ....

   7 They feed ....

Three pronouns are used to ask questions. They are called interrogative (questioning) pronouns. They are: **Who? Which? What?**
Complete the following, adding the correct interrogative pronouns:

C 1 ...*Who*......... are you? I am Moira.

   2 .... class are you in? I am in Class Two.

   3 .... is your name? My name is Moira O'Farrell.

These pronouns (called definite pronouns) answer the question 'Which?':
  this these that those

Complete the following, adding the correct definite pronouns:

D 1 Which cake is yours? ...*This*..... is my cake, ... cake is his.

   2 Which buns are yours? .... are our buns, ... buns are theirs.

★ Now test yourself in the use of pronouns

In the following there are groups of two words in the brackets. One of the words is correct, and the other is wrong. Cross out the wrong word.

A   1 (I, Me) listened to pop-music with (she, her).
    2 Her brother is taller than (we, us) are, but she is smaller than
       (I, me) am.
    3 Between you and (I, me) no one knows the secret.
    4 It is (they, them) we want to join the club.
    5 I know your face. (Who, What) is your name?
    6 (Who, Which) is writing his name in the book?
    7 The teacher knows (we, us) are sometimes annoyed with (us, ourselves).
    8 Was it (I, me) you saw at the party with (they, them)?
    9 (This, That) is your book here, and (this, that) is my book over there.
  10 Laura caught Becky and (she, her), but she did not catch Ann
      and (I, me).
  11 Nicholas is cleverer than (he, him) is, but not as clever as (I, me) am.
  12 This is the man (who, which) frightened (we, us).
  13 I played all day with (he, him) and (she, her).
  14 It curled (himself, itself) up and went to sleep.
  15 Those are (they, them).

From the evidence given at the trial of the Knave of Hearts in *Alice in Wonderland* by Lewis Carroll:

    1 They told me you had been to her,
    2 And mentioned me to him:
    3 She gave me a good character,
    4 But said I could not swim.
    5 He sent them word I had not gone,
    6 (We know it to be true:)
    7 If she should push the matter on,
    8 What would become of you?

B   Underline the 16 pronouns in the above verse.
C   Why is the passage so difficult to understand?

....

....

Adjectives

An adjective is a word that adds to the meaning of a noun. It is sometimes called a 'describing' word. These words are descriptive adjectives:

fat   soft   beautiful   cruel   hard-hearted   charming

Underline the descriptive adjectives in the following:

A 1 The <u>beautiful</u> princess helped the <u>frail old</u> man to rise.
   2 The cruel wolves tracked the wounded beast across the deep snow.
   3 Into the icy water the brave woman dived again and again.
   4 When the heavy lid was raised the brilliant jewels could be seen.
   5 The limping footballer scored the winning goal.

These are adjectives of quantity:
  Definite quantities: all the numerals (**one, two, three** and so on)
                         second, third, fourth and so on
                         both, double, treble and so on
  Indefinite quantities: **few, some, many, all, several, any**

Underline the adjectives of quantity in the following:

B 1 <u>Several</u> children took part in <u>both</u> plays.
   2 Some rain fell on the third day of the holidays.
   3 A few fish lurked under the second bridge.
   4 Many children had double helpings of chips.
   5 All pupils are expected to bring some toys to the fair.

Some adjectives put a limit on the noun.
Demonstrative adjectives **this   that   these   those**
  point out the object being talked or written about.
Interrogative adjectives **which   whose   what**
  ask questions about some object or person.
Distributive adjectives **each   every   either   neither   a   an   the**
  refer to individual objects or people.

Underline the limiting adjectives in the following:

C 1 <u>This</u> trophy belongs to <u>every</u> pupil.
   2 Neither child lives in that street.
   3 Which picture do you like best?
   4 Whose photograph hangs on the wall?
   5 The perfume costs a pound a fluid ounce.

Adjectives – degrees of comparison

The positive degree is the simple form of the adjective. It is the form shown in a dictionary entry: **cold beautiful callous swift great**

The comparative degree is used to compare two persons or two things:

Almost all adjectives of one syllable and many adjectives of two syllables form the comparative by adding **-r** or **-er** to the simple adjective.

cold becomes **colder**   **swift** becomes **swifter**   **great** becomes **greater**

Write the comparative form by the side of the simple adjective:

A   1 brave ....*braver*...... 2 quick .... 3 fine ....

4 short .... 5 large .... 6 small ....

7 narrow .... 8 pleasant .... 9 shallow ....

Some adjectives of two syllables also add **-r** or **-er**, but spelling rules mean that changes have to be made to the simple adjectives:

ugly becomes **uglier**   **thin** becomes **thinner**

Many adjectives of two syllables or more form the comparative by using **more** before the simple adjective:

careless becomes **more careless**   **beautiful** becomes **more beautiful**

The superlative degree is used in comparing three or more persons or things.

Almost all adjectives of one syllable and many of two syllables form the superlative by adding **-st** or **-est** to the simple adjective:

cold becomes **coldest swift** becomes **swiftest great** becomes **greatest**

Write by the side of the simple adjective the superlative form:

B   1 brave ....*bravest*...... 2 quick .... 3 fine ....

4 short .... 5 large .... 6 small ....

7 narrow .... 8 pleasant .... 9 shallow ....

Many adjectives of two syllables or more form the superlative by using **most** before the simple adjective:

Careless becomes **most careless**   **beautiful** becomes **most beautiful**

★ Now test yourself in the use of adjectives

Underline the adjectives in the following sentences:

A 1 The skilful driver kept his racing car steady on the slippery road.
   2 The kind lady dropped a small coin into the collecting box.
   3 The careless climber slipped from the narrow crumbling path.
   4 The fierce little creature attacked the terrified bird.
   5 Three boys and two girls ate several cakes each.
   6 Any pupil in the fourth year would envy those lucky boys.
   7 Some people with cold hands are supposed to have warm hearts.
   8 The thief – cold-blooded, cruel and greedy – killed the little dog.
   9 Each girl took every advantage of the holiday.
   10 Those earrings should not be worn at school.
   11 Whose work is this excellent picture?
   12 Which skates belong to neither girl?

Complete the following chart.

		Positive	Comparative	Superlative
B	1	mild	milder	mildest
	2	beautiful		
	3	rich		
	4	simple		
	5	benevolent		
	6	fierce		

Complete this chart which consists of adjectives compared irregularly.

C	1	little	less	least
	2	many, much		
	3	bad		
	4	good		
	5	far (for information)		
	6	far (distance)		

Verbs

The verb is an important part of the sentence. Nearly all sentences contain a verb.

A verb may express action, such as **swim, run, sing, fall, throw.**
It is therefore sometimes called the 'doing' word.

Underline the verb in the following.

A   1   Joanne <u>reads</u> the book.

         2   The boy danced on to the stage.

         3   The horse neighed.

         4   The tortoise crawled slowly across the stony path.

         5   With a splash the bucket dropped into the well.

         6   Stand to attention for the officer.

         7   Before the end of the concert the choir sang two ballads.

         8   The lightning flashed and the thunder clashed.

         9   The lion quietly stalks its prey.

     10   My mother wrote to the manager.

A verb may express a state of being, such as **is, are, am**. Other linking words that express a state or condition are **feel** (ill), **look** (smart), **taste** (sweet).

Underline the verb in the following:

B   1   The children <u>are</u> on the field.

         2   I am ready.

         3   The dog is in his kennel.

         4   The beaten team seems happy enough despite their defeat.

         5   The dogs are wild in the garden.

         6   The teacher sounds angry and the class grows quiet.

         7   Remain still until you are ready.

         8   The household guards look smart in their uniform.

         9   The battle seems lost.

     10   The umpire appears satisfied.

Auxiliary verbs

Sometimes we use two words to complete the verb. The lesser verbs that help the main verb are known as auxiliary verbs. Auxiliary verbs are: **is, are, was, were, may, might, should, would, will, shall, can, could, do, did, had, have, has.**

Underline the *two words* that complete the verb in the following:

A 1 The woman <u>has</u> <u>tried</u>.
   2 The ship will arrive.
   3 The boy might copy his neighbour's work.
   4 I shall run all the way to the station.
   5 The aircraft should land soon.
   6 The old man was injured in the road-accident.

The auxiliary verb may be separated from the main verb by another word or words.

> **The baby had never walked before.**
> **The driver can very rarely take passengers.**

Sometimes we need three words to complete a verb.

> **The wheel should be changed before Saturday.**
> **The pirate has been wounded by the sailor.**

Underline the verbs in the following:

B 1 The car <u>will</u> <u>be</u> <u>bought</u>.
   2 You should have waited for your little brother.
   3 The whistle had been blown before the goal was scored.
   4 The pony jumped the wall.
   5 The painting will be finished by morning.
   6 The painter had nearly finished her work.
   7 When the clock strikes nine the work will be done.
   8 The jockey whipped his horse.
   9 The lorry will go faster down the hill.
 10 Come along!
 11 You may want a new bike but you will never get it.
 12 Stand and deliver!

Number in the Verb – singular or plural

If the subject is singular (only one) the verb is singular.
If the subject is plural (more than one) the verb is plural.

> *Singular* (one only): I **walk**, you **walk**, he **walks**, she **walks**, it **walks.**
> *Plural* (more than one): we **walk**, you **walk**, they **walk**.

Complete the following using the correct number in the verb:

A 1   I play, he ...*plays*..., she ...*plays*..., it ..*plays*..., you ..*play*.., we ...*play*......

   2   I run, he runs, she ...., it ...., we ...., they ....

   3   I jump, he ...., she ...., it ...., we ...., they ....

   4   I fall, she ...., it ...., you ...., we ...., they ....

   5   I hit, he ...., she ...., you ...., they ...., we ....

   6   I ...., he writes, she ...., it ...., you ...., they ....

Note final **-es** (spelling rule)

   7   I catch, he catches, she ...., it ...., you ...., we ....

   8   I wish, he ...., she ...., you ...., we ...., they ....

Note change of final **-y** *to* **-ies** *in the third person singular (spelling rule)*

   9   I try, he tries, she ...., you ...., it ...., we ...., they ....

 10   I cry, he ...., she ...., you ...., we ...., they ....

Tenses in the Verb – present and past

The tense of a verb shows when an action takes place.
Present tense shows that an action takes place now or is completed now.

> she **walks**   she **is walk*ing***   she **has walked**   she **has been walk*ing***

Note the words ending in *-ing*. They are known as present participles
They show continuous action.
Past tense shows that an action took place yesterday or at some previous time.

> she **walk*ed***   she **was walking**   she **had walk*ed***   she **had been walking**

The simple past tense in regular verbs is formed by adding **-ed.**
The past participle, which ends in **-ed** or can be irregular (see page 18), shows completed action.

Principal parts of irregular verbs that cause trouble

Present	Past	Past participle	Present	Past	Past participle
am, be	was	been	give	gave	given
awake	awaked	awakened	go	went	gone
	awoke		grow	grew	grown
bear	bore	borne	hear	heard	heard
begin	began	begun	hide	hid	hidden
bend	bent	bent	kneel	knelt	knelt
bite	bit	bitten	know	knew	known
blow	blew	blown	lay	laid	laid
break	broke	broken	leave	left	left
bring	brought	brought	lose	lost	lost
catch	caught	caught	make	made	made
choose	chose	chosen	pay	paid	paid
come	came	come	ride	rode	ridden
do	did	done	ring	rang	rung
draw	drew	drawn	run	ran	run
drink	drank	drunk	say	said	said
eat	ate	eaten	sell	sold	sold
fall	fell	fallen	shake	shook	shaken
feel	felt	felt	sing	sang	sung
fly	flew	flown	swim	swam	swum
forget	forgot	forgotten	tear	tore	torn
freeze	froze	frozen	write	wrote	written
get	got	got			

Using the auxiliary verbs

Except for the simple present and the simple past tenses all tenses are formed with the auxiliary verbs **do, have, had, be, shall, will, should** and **would**. In speech, auxiliaries are often contracted (shortened).

is and **has** become **'s**   He's working   **She's** gone home.
had and **would** become **'d**   **He'd** scored. **She'd** often go to the pictures.

The negative is usually formed by adding not before the main verb.

I shall **not** go.   She was **not** playing.

In a dictionary, verbs are usually shown in their infinitive form:

(to) **catch**, (to) **shop**, (to) **fly**, (to) **learn**, (to) **forget**, (to) **hit**, (to) **mark,**
(to) **climb**

★ Now test yourself in the use of verbs

Underline the verbs in the following sentences:

A 1 The detective arrested the thief.
  2 In the murky water the diver fought the octopus.
  3 Kick the ball into the goal.
  4 The farmer ploughed the field in autumn.

B 1 They had caught the lost dog.
  2 I will telephone you in the morning.
  3 The most daring of the children would climb the tree.
  4 The team will be pleased with the result.

C 1 Once more the king is on the throne.
  2 The apple tastes sweet and the orange tastes bitter.
  3 If you feel ill tomorrow you will stay in bed.
  4 Now you are here I should really like you to stay.

Write the past tense of the following (you can use the chart on page 18):

D 1 bring .... 2 swim .... 3 kneel ....
  4 blow .... 5 say .... 6 lose ....

Write the past participle of the following:

E 1 draw .... 2 sell .... 3 lay ....
  4 break .... 5 fly .... 6 write ....

Fill each gap correctly with one of these words: know, known, knew, knows.

F 1 I .... the answer now.
  2 I .... yesterday that you were not well.
  3 I have .... the dog all my life.
  4 He .... his way to the market, and goes there every week.
  5 I will .... what to do when I see him tomorrow.
  6 I would like to .... her very much.

Adverbs

An adverb is a word that modifies or adds to the meaning of another word: a verb, an adjective or another verb.
Most adverbs are derived from adjectives by the addition of **-ly**.

    slow becomes **slowly**   **bad** becomes **badly**

Write the equivalent adverb for the following adverbs:

	Adjective	Adverb		Adjective	Adverb
A 1	quick	*quickly*	2	neat	....
3	loud	....	4	clear	....
5	free	....	6	brave	....

Sometimes the adverb is changed in spelling (see spelling rules).

Write the equivalent adjective for the following adverbs:

	Adjective	Adverb		Adjective	Adverb
B 1	*greedy*	greedily	2	....	easily
3	....	humbly	4	....	gently

Some adverbs do not end in -ly. They have the same form as adjectives.
Complete each sentence with the correct adverb:

	Adjective	Sentence with adverb
C 1	a *hard* job	I worked ......*hard*.......... to get the job finished.
2	an *early* train	The train arrived .... at the station.
3	a *fast* race	The girls ran .... to get there first.
4	a *short* stick	The wind made the ball fall .... of the goal.

Adverbs tell **how, when, where,** and **how much**.
Adverbs of manner answer the question **How?**
e.g. **badly, easily, slowly, well, surely, loudly, quietly, clumsily**

D 1 The children played ..*quietly*..... so that they should not disturb the sleeping man.

   2 Debbie fell .... off her bike and sprained her ankle.

   3 The knight shouted .... to make himself heard.

   4 The tortoise crawled .... but still won the race.

Adverbs of time answer the question **When?**

e.g. **today, soon, yesterday, before, now, since, seldom, often, immediately, already**

Complete each sentence with one of the adverbs listed above:

A 1 He came .....*yesterday*.......... and stayed the night.

2 Start .... the whistle is blown.

3 We have swimming .... and games tomorrow.

4 Comets .... appear in the sky.

5 The horse has .... won two races before this one.

6 I will run and .... catch him up.

Adverbs of place answer the question **Where?**

e.g. **here, everywhere, above, behind, outside, west, in, out, straight, nowhere**

Complete each sentence with one of the adverbs listed above:

B 1 He searched ....*everywhere*..... but could not find the treasure.

2 The wind blows .... but the hut is snug inside.

3 The arrow went .... to its target.

4 The bridesmaids followed close .... the bride.

5 He went in dry and came .... wet.

6 The church spire could be seen high .... the trees.

Adverbs of degree answer the question **How much?**

e.g. **almost, completely, less, thoroughly, quite, very, too, hardly, entirely, so**

Complete each sentence with one of the adverbs listed above:

C 1 The tired old man walked ....*very*........... slowly.

2 I have .... finished mowing the lawn and then I will rest.

3 When the boys are .... ready we will go.

4 I have .... money now I have finished shopping.

5 Dry your hair .... or you will catch cold.

6 Your work is .... good I am giving you full marks.

Interrogative adverbs are **When? Where? Why?** Relative adverbs are **when, where, why.**

Adverbs – degrees of comparison

Adverbs are compared in the same way as adjectives (see page 13).
The positive degree is the simplest form of the adverb. It is the form shown in a dictionary entry: **bravely   slowly   early   badly   much**

The comparative degree is used to compare two persons or things.
The superlative degree is used to compare three or more persons or things.

Adverbs of one syllable usually form the comparative degree by adding **-er** and the superlative degree by adding **-est**

Compare this chart:

	Positive	Comparative	Superlative
A 1	soon	sooner	soonest
2	hard		
3	fast		
4	late		
5	early		

Adverbs of two syllables or more generally form the comparative by adding **more** and the superlative by adding **most**

Compare this chart:

	Positive	Comparative	Superlative
B 1	briefly	more briefly	most briefly
2	happily		
3	quickly		
4	carefully		
5	easily		

Complete this chart of exceptions:

	Positive	Comparative	Superlative
C 1	badly, ill	worse	worst
2	far		
3	little		
4	much, many		
5	well		

★ Now test yourself in the use of adverbs

Underline the adverbs in the following:

A 1 The footballers will soon be ready and the match can begin.

2 The girl formerly lived with her grandmother.

3 The fox withdrew quickly into the wood.

4 The children behaved badly at the circus.

5 Jennifer once heard a mouse in the cupboard.

6 Where was the escaped prisoner hiding?

Complete the following with the adverbs from this list: **gleefully, impudently, smartly, bitterly, greedily, lovingly, fitfully, tunefully**

B 1 The cheeky girl answered .... 2 The sentry saluted ....

3 He chuckled .... 4 The hungry boy ate ....

5 The cat was caressed .... 6 The choir sang ....

7 The dog slept .... 8 The wind blew ....

Complete the following chart:

	Positive	Comparative	Superlative
C 1	willingly	....	....
2	ill	....	....
3	early	....	....
4	loudly	....	....
5	seriously	....	....
6	fearfully	....	....

Complete the following with the correct comparatives and superlatives of these adverbs: **closely, quickly, late, brightly, hard, carefully.**

D 1 You walked quickly but John walked ....

2 We both moved carefully, but I moved .... than you.

3 The lights shone brightly, but the stage lights shone ....

4 He looked at the insect closely, and then he looked .... still.

5 I tried hard, but Jill tried even ....

6 I came late, but Jamila was the .... to arrive.

Conjunctions

Conjunctions join together words or word groups.

Here are five simple conjunctions that are used to join together groups of words of equal value: **and but nor or yet**

Complete each of the following with the most suitable conjunction from the list above:

A 1 Katie ....*and*........ Maggie are friends.

   2 He was a giant, ... he was weak.

   3 The book was not on the shelves, ... was it on the desk.

   4 I will smile if I win .... if we lose.

   5 We quarrel .... we are friends.

Some conjunctions are used in pairs: **both ... and, so ... as, either ... or, neither ... nor, whether ... or**

Complete each of the following with the most suitable conjunction from the pairs listed above:

B 1 <u>Both</u> the highwayman ....*and*....... the innkeeper were guilty.

   2 The goal was missed by .... both the striker and the winger.

   3 Would you be so good .... to repeat the directions?

   4 Either you will confess .... I will tell the whole story.

   5 .... Freddie nor Lynn wants to go to the party.

   6 It does not matter to me whether you play .... not.

Underline both conjunctions in each sentence above.

Conjunctions can be grouped according to their special meanings.
They can express *Time, Place, Reason, Concession, Condition, Manner, Purpose, Result.*

Time **when while as since till until after before whenever**
Place **where wherever**
Reason **because since as**
Concession **although though while as even if whether ... or**
Condition **if unless**

Manner **as**   **as if**   **as ... as**   **so ... as**   **than**   **as though**
Purpose   **so that**
Result   **so ... that**

Complete the following sentences to make sense.
Underline the conjunctions.

A 1 <u>When</u> the pie was opened, the birds ....*began to sing*....................

   2 You must wash your hands before ....

   3 After you have eaten your supper ....

   4 I have not spoken to her since ....

   5 .... until you come.

   6 .... while the cat was asleep.

   7 As the dog barked ....

   8 I shall not see him till ....

B 1 He found the ball where ....

   2 Wherever the old man went ....

   3 I shall not come to the party because ....

   4 .... since you cannot hear.

   5 As it is Bonfire Night ....

C 1 I will not go to town even if ....

   2 Although she asked the pianist to play ....

   3 You will take part whether .... or not.

   4 Victoria will not swim in the pool unless ....

   5 If the shop is open ....

   6 I opened the gate into the field so that ....

   7 She acted her part as if ....

   8 As quick as lightning ....

Prepositions

Most prepositions are short words (**to, on, for**). Some prepositions are longer words (**underneath, alongside**). Some prepositions are even groups of words (**as far as, in spite of**).
Prepositions are normally placed before nouns or pronouns. They show the relation of one word (usually a noun or a pronoun) to some other word in the sentence.

The cat is **on** the mat. (**on** shows the position of the cat)
The cat walked **towards** its basket. (**towards** shows direction)
The cat goes out **after** dark. (**after** shows the time when the cat goes out)

The most common prepositions are:

up   down   in   on   at   with   of   for   over   by   between   towards   to

Complete the following adding the most suitable preposition from the list above.

A 1 We arrived ....*on*............ Monday.

  2 The girl curtseyed and gave the bouquet .... the queen.

  3 The ship sailed .... the desert island.

  4 The firemen slid .... the poles.

  5 The horse leapt .... the gate.

  6 Danny placed the cheese .... the two slices of bread.

  7 The mountaineer climbed .... the vertical cliff.

  8 The children swam .... the sea every day.

  9 The mermaid looked .... her reflection in the water.

Write three suitable and different prepositions for each sentence.

B 1 The book lay ....*in*............ the box.

  2 The book lay .... the box.

  3 The book lay .... the box.

  4 The skier raced .... the flags.

  5 The skier raced .... the flags.

  6 The skier raced .... the flags.

More prepositions

The following list consists of common prepositions:

about   after   from   to   within

Complete the following adding the most suitable preposition from each list:

A   1   The tortoise tucked its head ....*within*........ the shell.

    2   The boxer struck his opponent .... the bell sounded.

    3   The park is open .... dawn .... dusk.

    4   The mice ran .... the granary floor.

round   until   into   under   past

B   1   Gather ....*round*.......... and listen to my story.

    2   Go .... the wood .... you come to the blasted oak.

    3   It is now .... bedtime.

    4   You will find the house key .... the mat.

above   near   till   below   off

C   1   The stain can be seen ...*above*... the window but ......*below*........ the roof.

    2   We will not go home .... morning.

    3   The tiger is now .... the hunters.

    4   I switched .... the light and sat in the dark.

These are prepositions formed from groups of words:

because of   due to   except for   away from
on top of   in front of   by means of   out of

Complete the following from the list above:

D   1   I shall not come ......*because of*....... my mother's illness.

    2   All the children played .... Sam and Charles.

    3   This is the money .... you for meals.

    4   Do not stand .... the camera.

    5   Get .... the kicking horse or you will be hurt.

    6   The flag flew .... the church spire.

    7   I saw her when she came .... the shadows.

    8   They entered the castle .... the secret passage.

Interjections

The interjection is a word of exclamation that expresses emotion or feeling. It is sometimes shown by itself followed by an exclamation mark.

**Oh!   Ugh!   Nonsense!   Hooray!   Ah!   Ouch!   Ooh!   Oh dear!
Help!   Phew!   Oops!**

Complete the following adding the most suitable interjection from the list above:

A 1 ...._nonsense!_........ That was a silly remark to make.

   2 .... We have reached our destination at last.

   3 .... I'm very, very hot!

   4 .... You did surprise me.

   5 .... I am drowning!

The interjection is sometimes included in a sentence. It begins the sentence, and the exclamation mark comes at the end of the sentence. The interjection is followed by a comma, and the sentence explains the emotion – the reason for the exclamation.

Complete the following adding the most suitable interjection from the list at the top of the page:

B 1 ...._Ah!_..........., I can see you!

   2 ...., you kicked me!

   3 ...., I've dropped it!

   4 ...., what beautiful chocolates!

   5 ...., I think we're lost!

Articles

the is the definite article and is used for a particular thing.
a (before consonants) and **an** (before a vowel) are indefinite articles.

Complete this sentence:

C The clown climbed .... pole eating .... apple and .... banana.

★ Now test yourself in conjunctions, prepositions and interjections

Complete the following with the most suitable conjunction:

A 1 The horse galloped across the field .... jumped the gate.

2 The chairman spoke .... he closed the meeting.

3 You will wait here .... the order is given to go.

4 Post the notice .... everyone will be able to see it.

5 We must run .... we are late.

6 .... I have told her many times she still climbs the tree.

7 You must go .... you are invited or not.

8 Let me know .... you want to play.

9 The opossum can act .... it were dead.

10 The speaker shouted .... everyone in the vast crowd could hear.

Complete the following with the most suitable preposition:

A 1 The sailor swam .... the drowning man.

2 The boys climbed .... the greasy pole.

3 The tired old man leaned .... the wall.

4 The osprey dived .... the river and caught a fish.

5 The cashier placed the bags of money .... the counter.

6 The clown walked .... the tightrope.

7 The treasure was hidden .... the rubble.

8 The motor cyclist rode .... the wall of fire.

9 The paper was wrapped .... the parcel.

10 The dog jumped .... the fence and escaped.

Complete the following with the most suitable interjection:

C 1 ...., what a shock you gave me.

2 .... ! It is hot near the fire.

3 .... , that hurt!

4 .... ! I have forgotten to bring my money.

5 .... , we've won!

29

★ End-of-book test

Read this story:

A *little girl* was painting *industriously* a *picture* of her *favourite meal*. She *carefully painted* a *delicious plate* of *rich crisp chips, baked beans*, white and yellow *fried eggs* and *sizzling fat sausages*. The *teacher* said that she *could show* the picture to the *class* when she *had finished* it.

The girl painted until the picture *was finished*. Then she *proudly showed* the picture to the class. The class *gasped*, "Oh!" All the painting *was covered* with *red paint*.

"What a *terrible* thing *to do*!" said the teacher *angrily*. "Who *did* it?"

"I *did*," *said* the little girl. "It's *tomato sauce*. I always *have* lots of tomato sauce. I *love* it."

Write twelve nouns from the words in italics in the story above:

A 1 .... 2 .... 3 .... 4 ....

   5 .... 6 .... 7 .... 8 ....

   9 .... 10 .... 11 .... 12 ....

Write twelve verbs (some have more than one word) from the words in *italics* in the story:

B 1 .... 2 .... 3 .... 4 ....

   5 .... 6 .... 7 .... 8 ....

   9 .... 10 .... 11 .... 12 ....

Write twelve adjectives from the words in *italics* in the story above:

C 1 .... 2 .... 3 .... 4 ....

   5 .... 6 .... 7 .... 8 ....

   9 .... 10 .... 11 .... 12 ....

Write four adverbs from the words in *italics* in the story above:

D 1 .... 2 .... 3 .... 4 ....

Answers

Page 4

A   2. chair, cup, plate, spoon   3. park, ship, sand-castle, kite   4. William, John, Fred, Craig

B   2. horse   3. snake   4. frog   5. sparrow   6. lion

C   2. thief   3. children   4. goose   5. teeth   6. sheep

Page 5

A   2. goddess   3. grandmother   4. monk   5. bull   6. goose   7. empress   8. lord/gentleman   9. prince   10. wife

11. niece   12. son   13. ram   14. mare   15. bride   16. duke   17. landlord   18. aunt   19. daughter-in-law   20. heir

B   2. The queen awarded a medal to the heroine.   3. The bridesmaid followed the bride into the church.

4. The policewoman arrested the murderess.   5. The heiress to the whole estate was a penniless actress.

Page 6

A   Common gender: deer, singer, owner, passenger, explorer, swimmer, sheep, fowl, librarian, bird, people, animal, onlookers, choir, journalist, mob, reader, monarch, fish.

Neuter gender: house, mountain, volcano, window, pop-song, ladder, radio, boots, desk, book, ice-cream, road, sausage, balloon, rain, dagger, thunder, coal, car, canal, canoe, door, lemonade.

B   2. goose, gosling   3. pig, sow   4. dog, puppy   5. duck, duckling   6. stallion, foal   7. buck, doe   8. cow, calf   9. cock, chick

Page 7

A   2. crew   3. flock   4. company   5. gang   6. school   7. shoal   8. choir   9. stud   10. swarm

B   2. library   3. string   4. suit   5. bunch   6. chest   7. set   8. fleet   9. bundle   10. crate

Page 8. Now test yourself.

A   1. child   2. goose   3. box   4. man   5. passer-by   6. tooth

B   1. women   2. sheep   3. loaves   4. echoes   5. mouse-traps   6. feet

C   1. god   2. husband   3. bridegroom   4. emperor   5. nephew   6. male

D   1. lioness   2. aunt   3. witch   4. traitress   5. nun   6. headmistress

E   1. leopardess, cub   2. boar, piglet   3. ewe, lamb   4. bull, cow

F   1. army   2. herd   3. flock   4. pack   5. pride   6. gaggle   7. shoal   8. suite

G   1. audience   2. congregation   3. passengers   4. customers

H   1. hand   2. peal or ring   3. punnet   4. group

Page 9.

A   2. You   3. him   4. her   5. it   6. us   7. them

B   2. Yasmin plays tennis. She is good at the game.   3. The snake saw the bird. It glided away.

Page 10.

A   1. mine   2. yours   3. his   4. hers   5. his   6. ours   7. theirs

B   2. yourself   3. himself   4. herself   5. itself   6. ourselves   7. themselves

C   2. which   3. what

D   1. that   2. These, those

Page 11.

A   1. I, her   2. we, I   3. me   4. they   5. what   6. who   7. we, ourselves   8. me, them   9. this, that   10. her, me   11. he, I

12. who, us   13. him, her   14. itself   15. they

B   1. they, me, you, her   2. me, him   3. she, me   4. I   5. he, them, I   6. we, it   7. she   8. you

C   We do not know to what or to whom the pronouns apply.

Page 12.

A   2. cruel, wounded, deep   3. icy, brave   4. heavy, brilliant   5. limping, winning

B   2. some, third   3. few, second   4. many, double   5. All, some

C   2. Neither, that   3. Which   4. Whose   5. a

Page 13.

A   2. quicker   3. finer   4. shorter   5. larger   6. smaller   7. narrower   8. pleasanter   9. shallower

B   2. quickest   3. finest   4. shortest   5. largest   6. smallest   7. narrowest   8. pleasantest   9. shallowest

Page 14. Now test yourself.

A   1. skilful, racing, slippery   2. kind, small, collecting   3. careless, narrow, crumbling   4. fierce, little, terrified   5. three, two, several   6. any, fourth, those, lucky   7. some, cold, warm   8. cold-blooded, cruel, greedy, little   9. each, every

10. those, this   11. whose, excellent   12. which, neither.

B   2. more, most   3. richer, richest   4. simpler, simplest   5. more, most   6. fiercer, fiercest

C   2. more, most   3. worse, worst   4. better, best   5. further, furthest   6. farther, farthest

Page 15

A   2. danced   3. neighed   4. crawled   5. dropped   6. stand   7. sang   8. flashed, clashed   9. stalks   10. wrote

B   2. am   3. is   4. seems   5. are   6. sounds, grows   7. Remain, are   8. look   9. seems   10. appears

Page 16.

A   2. will arrive   3. might copy   4. shall run   5. should land   6. was injured

B   2. should have waited   3. had been blown, was scored   4. jumped   5. will be finished   6. had finished   7. strikes, will be done   8. whipped   9. will go   10. come   11. may want, will get   12. stand, deliver

Page 17.

A 2. runs, runs, run, run 3. jumps, jumps, jumps, jump, jump 4. falls, falls, fall, fall, fall 5. hits, hits, hit, hit, hit 6. write, writes, writes, write, write 7. catches, catches, catch, catch 8. wishes, wishes, wish, wish, wish 9. tries, try, tries, try, try 10. cries, cries, cry, cry, cry

Page 19. Now test yourself

A 1. arrested 2. fought 3. kick 4. ploughed

B 1. had caught 2. will telephone 3. would climb 4. will be pleased

C 1. is 2. tastes, tastes 3. feel ill, will stay 4. are, should like, to stay

D 1. brought 2. swam 3. knelt 4. blew 5. said 6. lost

E 1. drawn 2. sold 3. laid 4. broken 5. flown 6. written

F 1. know 2. knew 3. known 4. knows 5. know 6.know

Page 20.

A 2. neatly 3. loudly 4. clearly 5. freely 6. bravely

B 2. easy 3 humble 4. gentle

C 2. early 3. fast 4. short

D 2. clumsily 3. loudly 4. slowly

Page 21.

A 2. immediately 3. today 4. seldom 5. already 6. soon

B 2. outside 3. straight 4. behind 5. out 6. above

C 2. almost 3. quite/completely 4. less 5. thoroughly 6. so

Page 22.

A 2. harder, hardest 3. faster, fastest 4. later, latest 5. earlier, earliest

B 2. more happily, most happily 3. more quickly, most quickly 4. more carefully, most carefully 5. more easily, most easily

C 2. farther, farthest 3. less, least 4. more, most 5. better, best

Page 23.

A 1. soon 2. formerly 3. quickly 4. badly 5. once 6. where

B 1. impudently 2. smartly 3. gleefully 4. greedily 5. lovingly 6. tunefully 7. fitfully 8. bitterly

C 1. more, most 2. iller, illest; or worse, worst 3. earlier, earliest 4. more, most 5. more, most 6. more, most

D 1. more quickly 2. more carefully 3. brightest 4. more closely 5. harder 6. latest

Page 24.

A 2. but 3. nor 4. or 5. but/yet

B 2. both, and 3. so, as 4. Either, or 5. Neither, nor 6. Whether, or

Page 25.

A 2.before 3. After 4. since 5. until 6. While 7. As 8. till

B 1. Where 2. Wherever 3. because 4. since 5. As

C 1. even if 2. Although 3. whether 4. unless 5. If 6. so that 7. as if 8. As … as

Page 26

A 2. to 3. towards 4. down 5. over 6. between 7. up/down 8. in 9. at

B 2/3. on/by 4/5/6. towards/between/through

Page 27

A 2. after 3. from/to 4. about

B 2. into, until 3. past 4. under

C 2. till 3. near 4. off

D 2. except for 3. due to 4. in front of 5. away from 6. on top of 7. out of 8. by means of

Page 28

A 2. Hooray! 3. Oh dear! 4. Oh! 5. Help!

B 2. Ouch 3. Oops 4. Ooh 5. Oh dear

C the, an, a

Page 29. Now test yourself.

A 1. and 2. before 3. until 4. where 5. because 6. although (though) 7. whether 8. if 9. as if 10. so that

B 1. to 2. up 3. against 4. into 5. on 6. along 7. beneath (under, underneath) 8. through 9. round 10. over

C 1. Oh 2. Phew 3. Ouch 4. Oh 5. Hooray

Page 30. Now test yourself.

Count five points for each correct answer. You could score 200 points for all-correct answers.

Nouns A 1. girl 2. picture 3. meal 4. plate 5. chips 6. beans 7. eggs 8. sausages 9. teacher 10. class 11. paint 12. sauce.

Verbs B 1. painted 2. could show 3. had finished 4. was finished 5. showed 6. gasped 7. was covered 8. to do 9. did 10. said 11. have 12. love

Adjectives C 1. little 2. favourite 3. delicious 4. rich 5. crisp 6. baked 7. fried 8. sizzling 9. fat 10. red 11. terrible 12. tomato

Adverbs D 1. industriously 2. carefully 3. proudly 4. angrily